7 Duets for Piano

Swing Band Dance Hits

Arranged by
Jim Lyke

Edited by
Robert Pace

CD Included

Thanks to Lee Evans for his musical suggestions and to Paul Sheftel for his assistance with the CD recording.

SWING BAND DANCE HITS FOR PIANO DUET
CD TRACKS

I'M JUST WILD ABOUT HARRY
Track 1   Primo and Secondo
Track 2   Primo
Track 3   Secondo

MARGIE
Track 4   Primo and Secondo
Track 5   Primo
Track 6   Secondo

LOVESICK BLUES
Track 7   Primo and Secondo
Track 8   Primo
Track 9   Secondo

WAY DOWN YONDER IN NEW ORLEANS
Track 10   Primo and Secondo
Track 11   Primo
Track 12   Secondo

STUMBLING
Track 13   Primo and Secondo
Track 14   Primo
Track 15   Secondo

CHICAGO
Track 16   Primo and Secondo
Track 17   Primo
Track 18   Secondo

THE JAPANESE SANDMAN
Track 19   Primo and Secondo
Track 20   Primo
Track 21   Secondo

I'M JUST WILD ABOUT HARRY

Secondo

words and music by
Noble Sissle and Eubie Blake
arranged by Jim Lyke

Spirited ♩ = 112 (♫ = ♪)

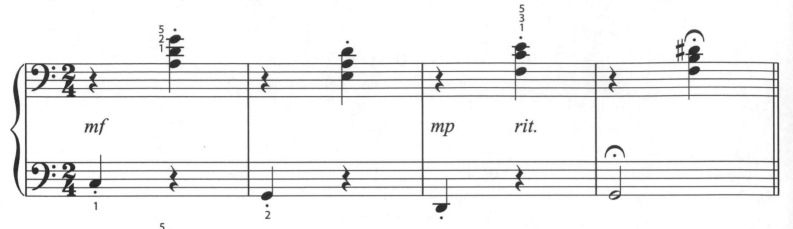

heavn' - ly bliss - es of his kis - ses

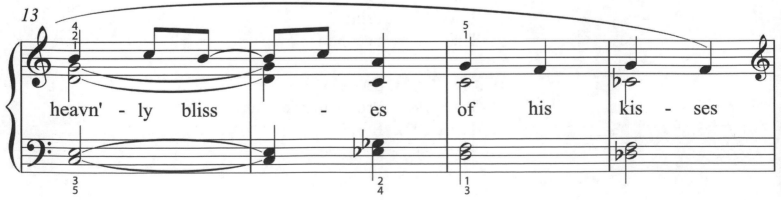

I'M JUST WILD ABOUT HARRY

Primo

words and music by
Noble Sissle and Eubie Blake
arranged by Jim Lyke

Secondo

fill   me   with   ec   -   sta   -   cy_____   He's

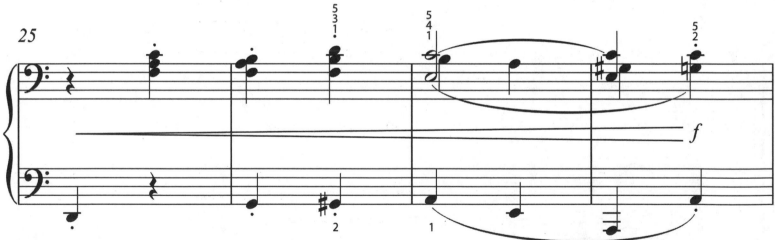

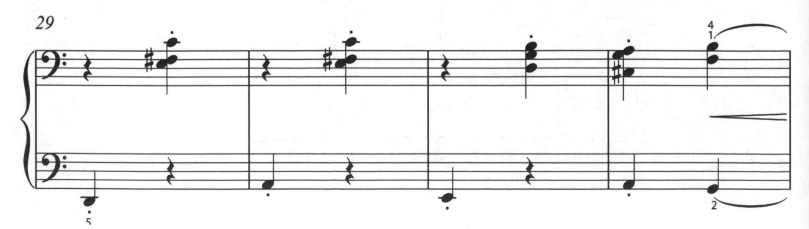

Primo

Secondo

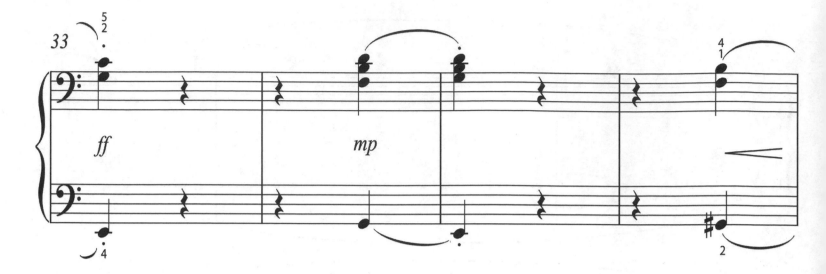

Primo

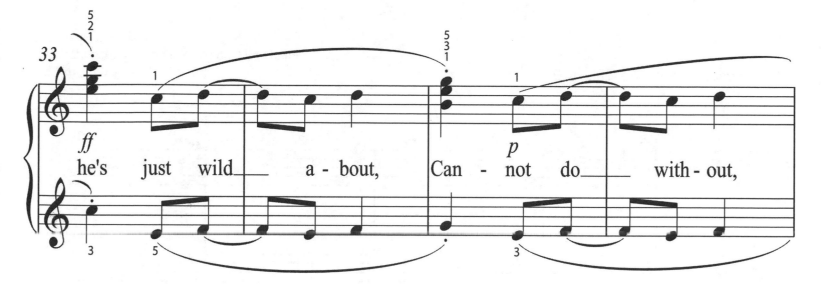

33

ff

he's   just   wild____   a - bout,   Can - not   do____   with - out,

p

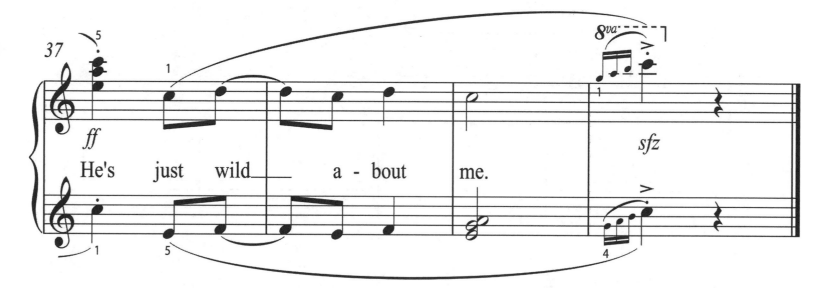

37

ff

He's   just   wild____   a - bout   me.

sfz

MARGIE

Secondo

words by Benny Davis
music by Con Conrad and J. Russell Robinson
arranged by Jim Lyke

MARGIE

Primo

words by Benny Davis
music by Con Conrad and J. Russell Robinson
arranged by Jim Lyke

Moderately bright ♩ = 100-110

My lit - tle

Mar - gie, I'm al - ways think-ing of you,

Mar - gie, I'll tell the world I love you.

Don't for - get your prom-ise to me.

Secondo

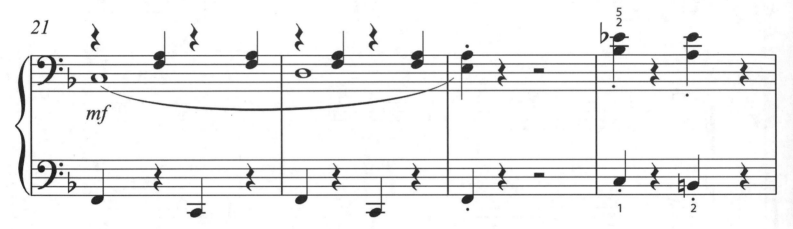

all is said and done, there is real - ly on - ly one,____

Primo

14

Secondo

Primo

Mar - gie, Mar - gie, it's you.

you.

LOVESICK BLUES
Secondo

words and music by Irving Mills
and Cliffor Friend
arranged by Jim Lyke

Moderate Swing ♩ = 126

That long last   day we spent a - lone.   I'm   yearn-ing for it

LOVESICK BLUES

Primo

words and music by Irving Mills
and Cliffor Friend
arranged by Jim Lyke

Moderate Swing ♩ = 126

(loco)

Got the feel-ing called the "Blue Hoo's"____ since my Sweet-ie said "Good - Bye"____ Seems I don't know what to "Doo - Hoo"____ All day long I sit and cry____

2428

Secondo

yet_____ She thrilled me, filled me, with a kind of lov- in',

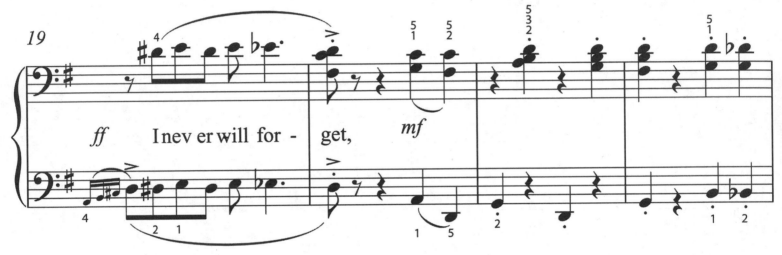

ff I nev er will for - get, *mf*

f

Primo

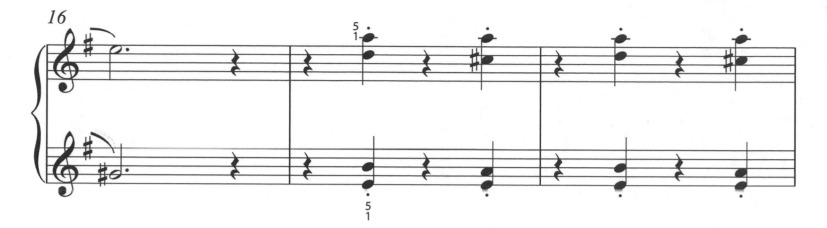

the way she called me "sweet dad-dy"   'Twas just a beau-ti-ful

dream____   I hate to think it's all - ov - er____   I lost my heart it

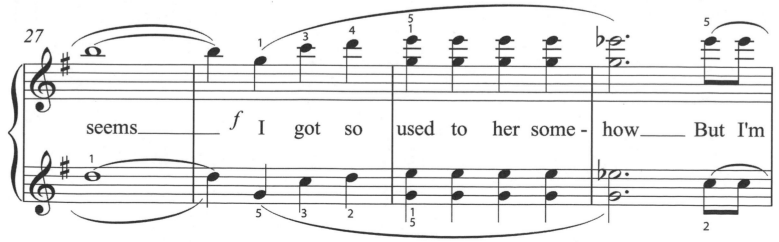

seems____   I got so used to her some - how____ But I'm

Secondo

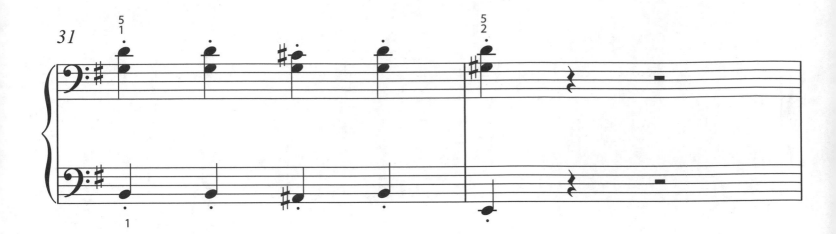

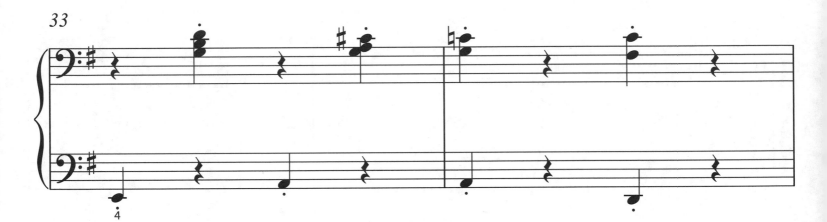

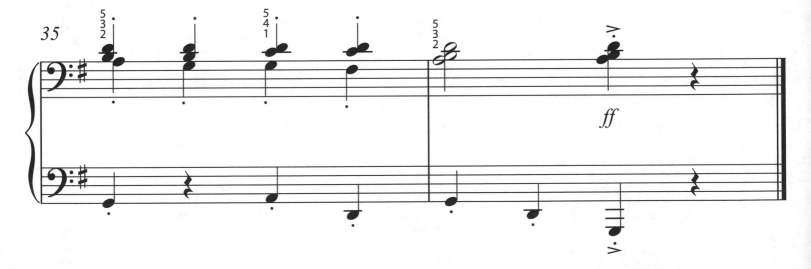

Primo

WAY DOWN YONDER IN NEW ORLEANS

Secondo

words and music by
Henry Creamer and J. Layton Turner
arranged by Jim Lyke

Medium Swing   ♩ = 130

2428

WAY DOWN YONDER IN NEW ORLEANS

Primo

words and music by
Henry Creamer and J. Layton Turner
arranged by Jim Lyke

Secondo

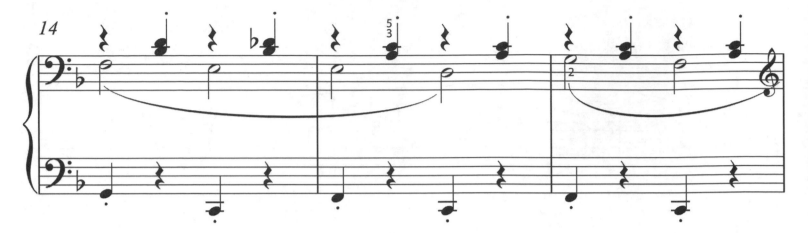

f Stop! Oh, won't you give your la-dy fair___ a lit-tle smile___

Stop! You bet your life you'll lin-ger there___ a lit-tle

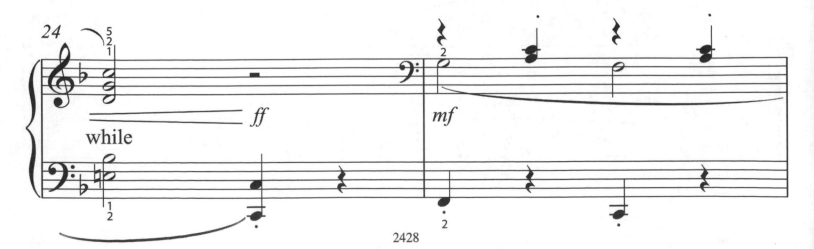

while

Primo

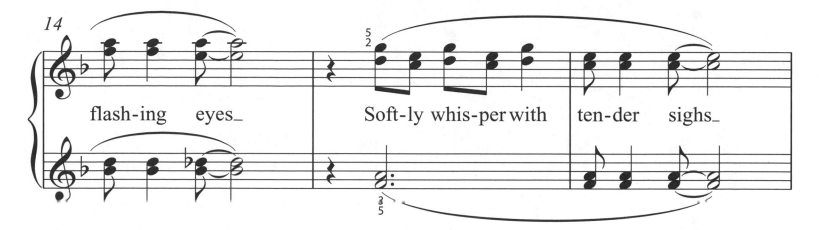

flash-ing eyes_ Soft-ly whis-per with ten-der sighs_

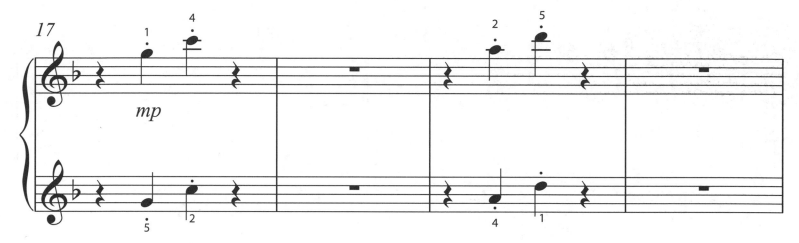

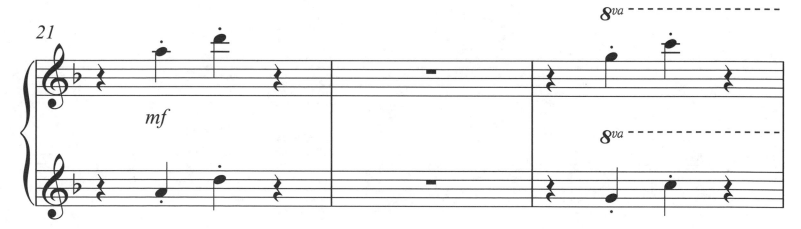

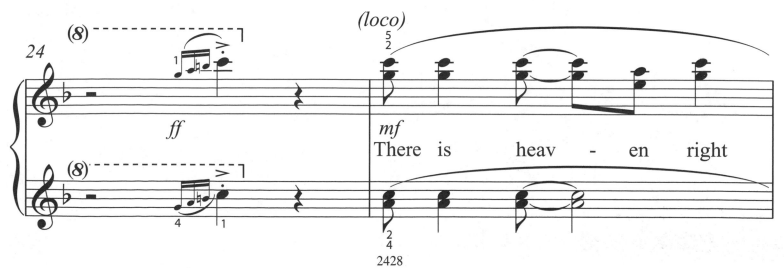

There is heav - en right

2428

Secondo

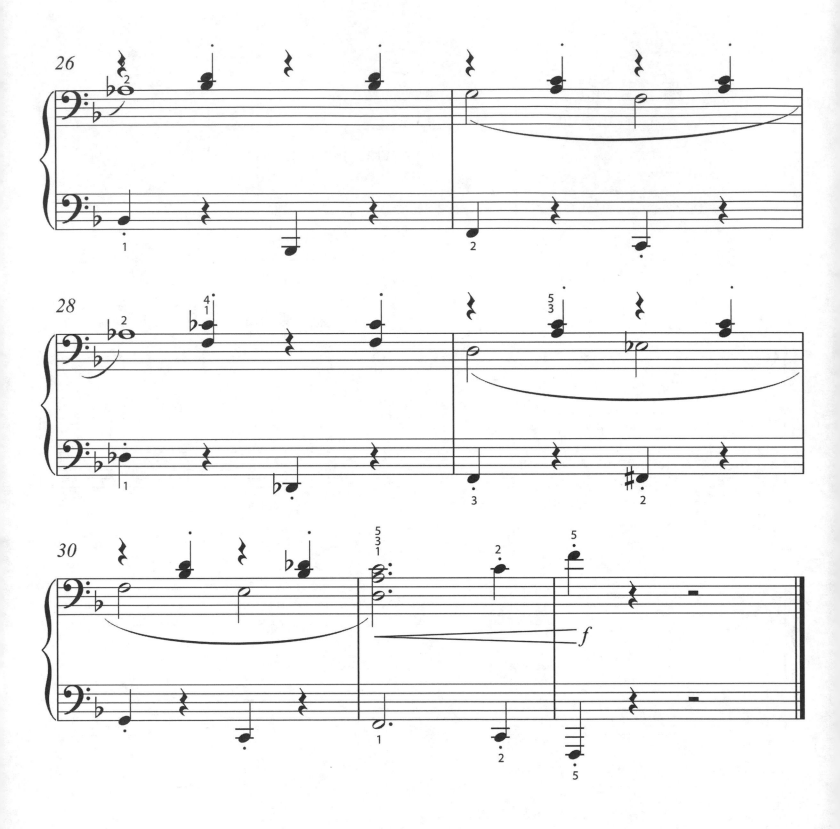

Primo

here on earth

With those beau - ti - ful

queens

Way down yon - der in

New Or - leans.

f

STUMBLING
Secondo

words and music by Zez Confrey
arranged by Jim Lyke

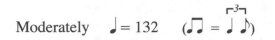

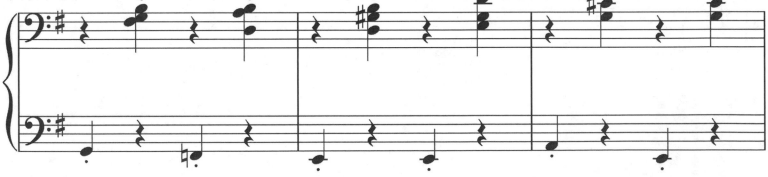

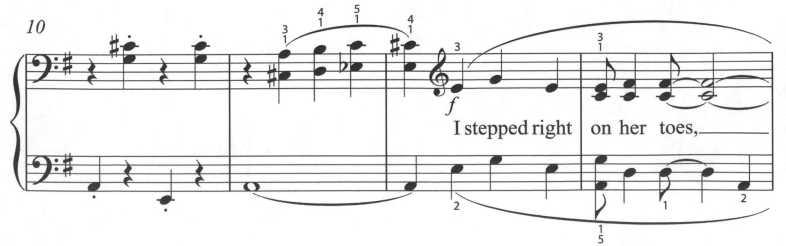

I stepped right on her toes,

STUMBLING
Primo

words and music by Zez Confrey
arranged by Jim Lyke

2428

30

Secondo

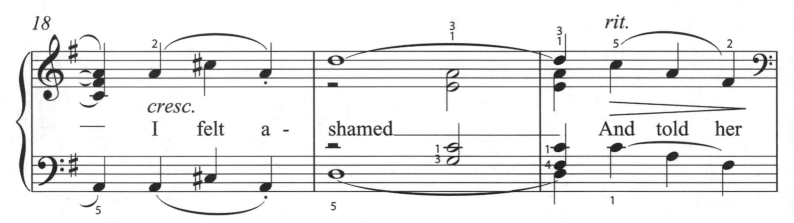

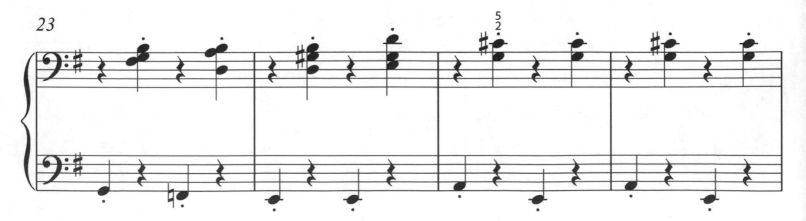

2428

Primo

Secondo

Primo

CHICAGO
Secondo

words and music by Fred Fisher
arranged by Jim Lyke

bet your bot-tom dol -lar   you

CHICAGO

Primo

words and music by Fred Fisher
arranged by Jim Lyke

Moderato ♩ = 63   Very Rhythmic

mf   **f** Chi-

ca-go,___ Chi-ca-go,___ that tod-dl'-ing town,___

tod-dl'-ing town, Chi-ca-go,___ Chi-ca-go,___ I'll

show you a-round,   I love it,   bet your bot-tom dol-lar   you

2428

Secondo

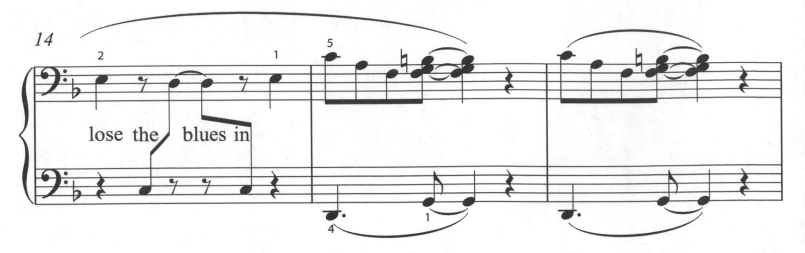

lose the blues in

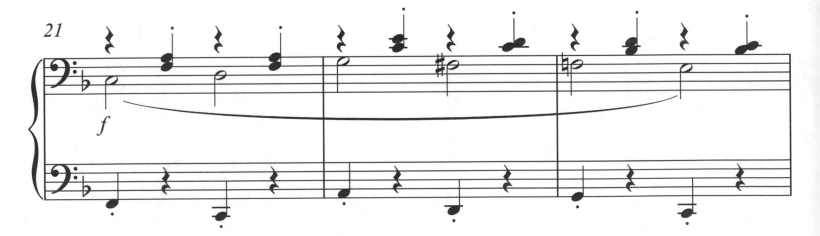

Primo

38

Secondo

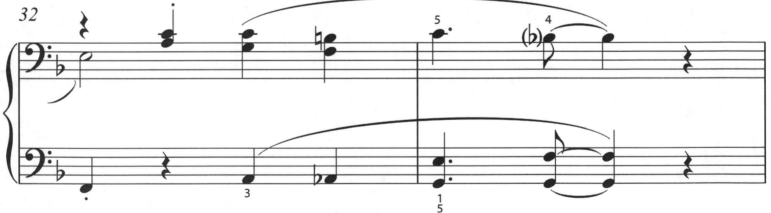

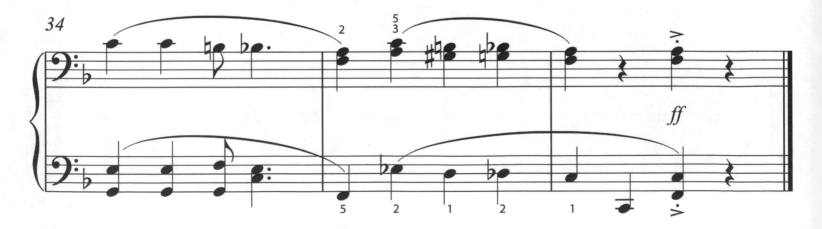

Primo

THE JAPANESE SANDMAN

Secondo

words and music by Zez Confrey
arranged by Jim Lyke

Moderately   ♩ = 120   (♫ = ♫)

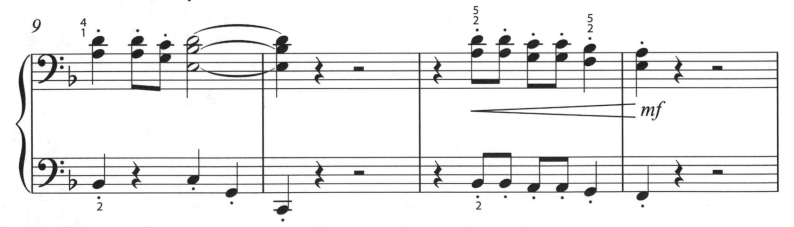

2428

THE JAPANESE SANDMAN

Primo

words and music by Zez Confrey
arranged by Jim Lyke

42

Secondo

Primo

2428

44

30

33

Primo

Trade him sil - ver for gold,_____ Just an old sec-ond

hand man,_____ Trad-ing new days for old.

THE SWING BAND ERA

Big band jazz had its origins in smaller jazz ensembles that evolved in the 1920s. The term "swing band" was applied to big bands beginning in the 1930s. These bands often played in major hotels whose ballrooms were venues for social dancing. Big bands also played at outdoor pavilions in amusement parks for dancing in the 1930s and 1940s and beyond. Other venues included college gymnasiums for events such as proms. A famous ballroom in Harlem, The Savoy, was well known for new dance styles such as the Lindy Hop.

The instrumentation of a big band (sometimes called jazz band, jazz orchestra or dance band) usually consisted of 12 to 19 instrumentalists who played saxophones and brass instruments, plus a rhythm section consisting of a piano, guitar, bass and drums. Arrangers were important to the big band. Improvised solos were common.

Early important band leaders such as Paul Whiteman employed famous musicians such as the legendary cornetist Bix Beiderbecke. Singers were hired to put across the latest song hits. One of Whiteman's singers was Bing Crosby who went on to a major career in films. Two cities flourished with big bands: Kansas City and New York City. Kansas City promoted a "bluesy" style while New York tended to be more sophisticated and was known for "hot jazz." Major black bands in the 1930s and beyond included those of Duke Ellington, Cab Calloway, Count Basie and Chick Webb. The white bands of Benny Goodman, Artie Shaw, Tommy Dorsey and Glenn Miller became very popular with dancers and listeners. Big bands made frequent radio broadcasts and theater appearances.

Each band employed one or more jazz vocalists. Frank Sinatra sang at various times with both the Harry James and Tommy Dorsey bands. Peggy Lee sang with the Benny Goodman band. Other prominent vocalists during the big band era included such well known singers as Doris Day, Ella Fitzgerald, Mildred Bailey, Dick Haymes, Rosemary Clooney, Jo Stafford and Margaret Whiting. As with Frank Sinatra, many of these vocalists left the big band business for careers in film, cabaret, theater and concert appearances.

COMPOSER AND LYRICIST NOTES

Eubie Blake (1883-1983) and **Noble Sissle** (1889-1975) who wrote **I'm Just Wild About Harry**, were a successful song writing team who broke the black color barrier on Broadway with their show, **Shuffle Along.** Besides composing, Blake was a renowned ragtime pianist. In addition to lyric writing, Sissle led orchestras. Blake received the Presidential Medal of Honor in 1981 from President Reagan.

Con Conrad (1881-1938) and **J. Russell Robinson** (1892-1963) who wrote **Margie,** had a hit on their hands with a song made popular by dance bands and one used in several movies. Con Conrad's celebrated song, **The Continental** was used in a Ginger Rogers and Fred Astaire movie in the mid 1930's.

Irving Mills (1874-1985) and **Clifford Friend** (1892-1963) who wrote **Lovesick Blues,** were both composers and lyricists. Mills wore many hats. He was a publisher, orchestra leader, recording company owner and promoter of the early careers of band leaders Duke Ellington and Cab Calloway.

Henry Creamer (1879-1930) and **J. Turner Layton** (1894-1978) who wrote **Way Down Yonder In New Orleans,** were African American songwriters who sang, danced and worked as a team in Vaudeville. They contributed songs to various Broadway shows and reviews.

Zez Confrey (1895-1971) who wrote **Stumbling,** was a composer of "novelty piano" pieces such as **Dizzy Fingers** and **Kitten On The Keys.** He was something of a musical phenomenon, well trained at the Chicago Musical College, and later in his life wrote for Big Bands. In 1924, he was featured in the same concert where Gershwin's **Rhapsody In Blue** was introduced.

Fred Fisher (1875-1942) who wrote **Chicago,** was both a composer and lyricist. He also wrote the enduring tune, **Peg 0' My Heart.** He was known for his quirky rhythms made to fit his lyrics. Other geographic songs he wrote besides Chicago include **Norway** and **Siam.**

Richard Whiting ((1891-1938) and **Raymond B. Egan** (1890-1952) who wrote **The Japanese Sandman,** were a successful team in Hollywood. Whiting, as composer, worked for many studios. An early hit (with Egan), **Till We Meet Again,** sold over 7 million copies. Other successful movie songs by this team include **Ain't We Got Fun,** and **Sleepy Time Gal.** Two other well known songs of Whiting include **You're Just Too Marvelous** and **Hooray For Hollywood.**